AD WAMMES

TOCCATINA

MUSIC DEPARTMENT

OXFORD
UNIVERSITY PRESS

to Willem van Twillert

Toccatina

AD WAMMES

I: Octave 4', Rohrflöte 4'
II: Spitzflöte 4'
Ped.: Gedackt 8'
Add I+II coupler if I is unenclosed

Composer's note: The suggested registrations are based upon the possibilities of my Clavia Nord C2 organ. You are welcome to adapt the registrations where necessary.

Printed in Great Britain

OXFORD UNIVERSITY PRESS, MUSIC DEPARTMENT, GREAT CLARENDON STREET, OXFORD OX2 6DP

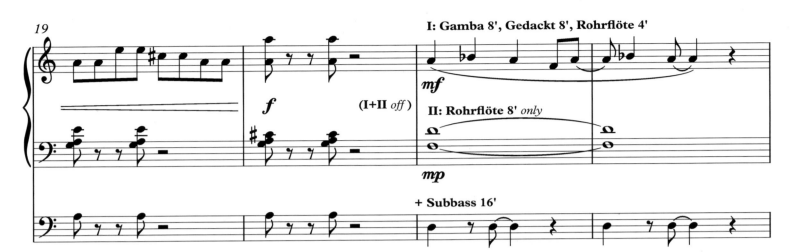

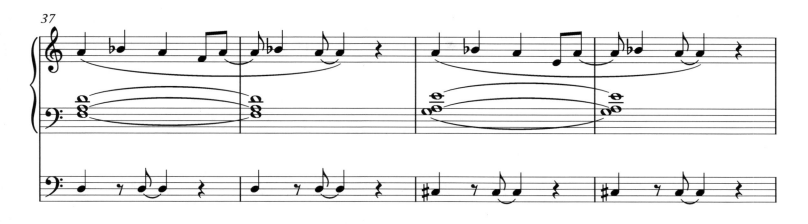

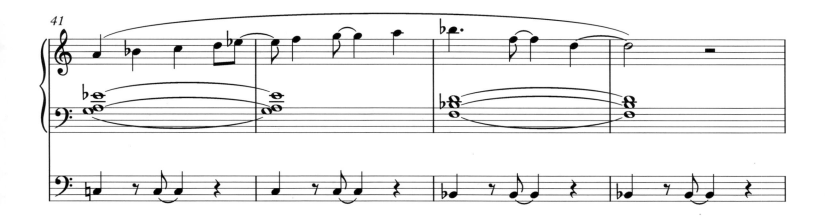

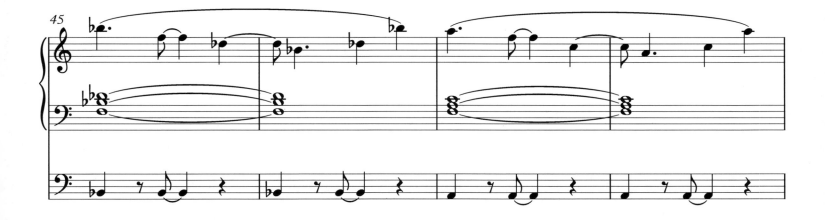

+ Spitzflöte 4'

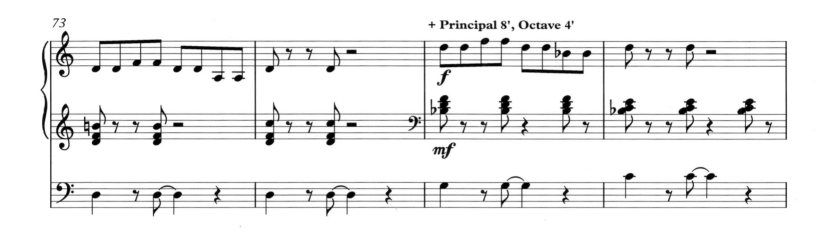

+ Principal 8', Octave 4'

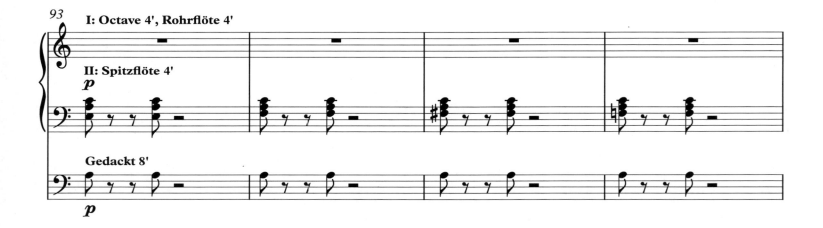